GREAT

EXPECTATIONS

A Faith Requirement

Dr Claudette King

ISBN:10: 1475046855
ISBN-13:978-1475046854

,

DEDICATION & THANKS

To Evadney Brown, affectionately called Sanie, my step-mother, words cannot describe just how much I love and appreciate you for all that you have instilled in me from a child. The foundation you laid stands as a monument of who I am today.
Thank you

To Shirley Barrett & Rosemarie Miller two of my best friends, thanks for all your support, encouragement, and love.

To Inez, Monica, Stacey, Nordia and Krystal my sisters and Claude, David and Oral my brothers, I love you all for in your varied ways, you have all taught me something and left an indelible print upon my life.

CONTENTS

ACKNOWLEDGEMENTS

GOD!!!

You are the lover of my soul

CHAPTER 1

IDENTIFY YOUR EXPECTATIONS

What is that you have in your hand?

^{1}*Job 5:27*

Job 5:27   **Lo this, we have searched it, so it is; hear it, and know thou it for thy good.**

From July through to October 2011, I conducted a seminar called "Order in the Church" at various locations across the United Kingdom. I began each session by

---

^{1} E-Sword KJV

asking those in attendance to first note down on a piece of paper, what it was they hoped to gain from the session.   This was because I believed that in order to measure satisfaction, expectations must first be identified.   There is no way you will be able to know if I have satisfied your anticipations without prior knowledge of what it is you are expecting.

Today, we hear the terminology "Managing Expectations" used quite often in the work place. This is largely due to the realization that many employees get disgruntled in their role, disappointed that the company is not meeting their perceived idea of what working at that company would have been like. Managers and supervisors are now taking a new approach to dealing with employees' expectations. Whether it is a new role, a pay rise or a training and development workshop; employees are first given the aims and objectives of what they are about to embark on, thereby ensuring that everyone is beginning with the same goal in mind.   To manage expectations requires that the expectations are known or identified and prior agreement takes place.

When we look then at identifying expectations, one must know what it is they are expecting. Be it from life, from God, from others; or from ourselves. This is a necessary criteria.

On many occasions, people of all classes and backgrounds have embarked upon a quest. An expedition of discovery, to uncover or discover as it were, something about themselves or someone else.

Such searches, prior to commencement; will necessitate the individual or group conducting the exploration to first know what it is they are looking for. Initially recognizing this is imperative, as ignorance regarding what is being sought, may lead to missing or not realising when your search has concluded, for the thing you were searching for has been found.

Every relationship regardless of the parties involved comes with expectations, only after these are clearly identified can they be managed. There are times when what we are expecting someone else to do is simply outside of their scope and therefore, they will not be able to perform that task, thereby, leaving others dissatisfied, due to the fact that what they were expecting to receive and what was finally delivered was not cohesive.

Unmet expectations are often or usually the cause of conflict and strife. The reverse is true, identified expectations lead to satisfaction. It therefore cannot be over-emphasised how important it is to pinpoint what will be expected before embarking on any venture.

Summary

Faith requires the same intent, for too often our prayers seem to go unanswered, but is that really the case or is it that we did not specify what we were praying for, we were not explicit in our request but were rather vague, asking for *anything* instead of something specific.

Before we agree anything, it is imperative that we know exactly what both parties or all those involved are expecting. Whether in a marriage, an event, a job, a trip, or a relationship it is imperative to identify expectations and agree.

CHAPTER 2

PREPARE YOUR EXPECTATIONS
Preparation is the key to success

[2] 1 Corinthians 9:24 -26

1Co 9:24 Know ye not that they which run in a race run all, but one receiveth the prize? So run, that ye may obtain.

1Co 9:25 And every man that striveth for the mastery is temperate in all things. Now they do it to obtain a corruptible crown; but we an incorruptible.

1Co 9:26 I therefore so run, not as uncertainly; so fight I, not as one that beateth the air:

---

[2] E-Sword KJV

During my high school years I was one of the top athletes in my school. I competed in several track and field events, such as one hundred and ten meters hurdle, two hundred, four hundred, eight and fifteen hundred meters race, relays, high jump and long jump.

Being involved in sports meant rigid training as opportunities to compete came often. I competed in the school's sports day and also represented the school at girls championships, SDC Relays and other sporting events. I was even approached about running for Jamaica, back in my hay-day.

Those were the days; I earned respect at my school, because my name was amongst those printed in the schools magazines and other publications featuring upcoming events. To gain the support of parents and non-competing students, the magazines were distributed to the entire school informing them of each event, while extending an invitation for them to cheer us on.

However, prior to the actual event, rigorous training was necessary. Yes competing at the event and carrying the responsibility of representing the school was great, but every athlete knew the extensive training and preparation that was pivotal, and the painstaking hours it took.

Eating the right foods, drinking high energy drinks, ensuring that you got enough rest, and staying away from activities that exerted too much energy, especially prior to an event.

Because I was serious about competing, you would not find me strolling to the mall to look at the latest clothes and handbag collections. I did not know the latest designer clothing, neither had I attended the latest celebrity concert. For my entire spare time, was spent on the track, training, preparing and planning for the next sporting event.

My trainer at the time was Mr Turner, a tall well-built man with a stern look and authoritarian approach. We were not allowed to arrive late for practice, and if we did, we would end up having to count a few extra laps on the warm up. We did not answer back when Mr Turner issued instructions, for that would earn us a few extra push ups, neither did we miss practice without a valid, justified reason; it was simply unacceptable.

His regime was harsh, but it yielded results. He would increase the speed of the slower girls by putting them to race with those who were knowingly faster. His aim was to have you chase them until your time increased and eventually you ran the risk of catching or passing them, harsh but effective. I know this for as a little girl my older brothers would normally give a head start whenever we raced; but after I started training, they had to run flat out to beat me, of course the head start was abolished.

Training was every day after school and it increased to include weekends as events drew closer. Sometimes a group of us would go to the beach not to swim, but to run in the wet sand, for a different terrain or in the water, building resistance, forcing us to push through and keep up our speed.

Now all this preparation was being done with a view that I should be the best when I attended for the race. It created an expectation; because I had prepared my body, and trained extensively. I am in tip-top shape and ready to perform to the best of my ability. My intention was to win the race, no matter who was standing at the starting line with me, because I had prepared. When that umpire says, "*on your marks, get set*" the anticipation of hearing the word "*go*" or the sounding of the gun, indicating that I can begin running was overwhelming, the excitement and adrenaline builds up in me like a ball, spinning and fizzing to the surface.

When I hear the sound, off I go, speeding to the finish line with all my might, strength and vigour, for the many months of preparation and hard work is expected to now pay off.

Arms swinging, feet spinning and head bobbing I chase to the finish line, trying to stay ahead of the competition, for I have prepared for the race and the expectation of winning is great. Due to the fact that I underwent such extensive preparation, I had my mind set on the prize, I was not merely going out there to run, but rather to take the prize and come away the victor.

This is what Paul was saying to us in 1 Corinthians 9:24-26. He is admonishing us to run as one that takes home the prize, what Paul did not detail is the preparation necessary prior to the race.

No serious athlete will ever attend for a race without prior preparation. That kind of risk is far too great. For when you run with all that you have, you are exerting pressure on your heart, requiring it to pump blood around the body faster, you are placing stress on your muscles, those in your legs, arms and torso (yes, you use the core muscles of your torso as well). Just going to race without any kind of preparation will leave you with aches and pains and you definitely cannot expect to win when you haven't done the prior work.

The Christian race requires spiritual preparation in order to endure and to win. No child of God can enter this race without faith, furthermore, to win or even to endure necessitates faith. Hebrews 11:6 warns us that without faith it is impossible to please Him (God) for he that comes to God must (1) believe that God is. The individual that will approach the invisible God believing though he cannot be seen with the eye or heard with the ear, nor smelled with the nostrils or touched with the hands or tasted by the tongue, yet know and accept of a surety that God is, and also that God rewards them who diligently seek him. This kind of approach demands faith.

> [3]*Heb 11:6 But without faith it is impossible to please him: for he that cometh to God must believe that he is, and that he is a rewarder of them that diligently seek him*

Expectation comes when you have faith and faith comes through knowledge. Romans 10:17 tells us that faith comes by hearing, but hearing what? The Word of God. The Word of God brings knowledge about God, and knowing God, allows you to expect him to work according to his word.

> [4]*Roms 10:17   So then faith cometh by hearing and hearing by the word of God.*

---

[3] E-Sword KJV
[4] E-Sword KJV

If you do not expect something, then you won't be anticipating it, so if it shows up, you will either, (1) miss it, or (2) be surprised by it; for you were not looking for it; therefore you were not prepared to receive it.

Summary

Faith then requires you to have done some preparation. James says it well, he said, show me your faith without your works, and I will show you my faith, by my works.

> [5]*Jas 2:18*   *Yea, a man may say, Thou hast faith, and I have works: shew me thy faith without thy works, and I will shew thee my faith by my works.*

Because you have faith, you will do the necessary work or preparation. Preparation will birth expectation, and expectation will propel you into a posture to receive.

A few months ago I heard a story from a minister at my church. He told how a particular village was suffering from a drought and longed for rain. The

---

[5] E-Sword KJV

people decided to pray for rain. They planned a prayer day and a prayer point to meet, which was atop of a hill and there they would pray to God, for him to send rain. While they were there praying, it began to rain but only one little boy had actually carried his umbrella.

CHAPTER 3

ALIGN YOUR EXPECTATIONS

*The safest place in the whole wide world
is in obedience to the will of God*

[6]Ephesians 4:13

Eph 4:13   *Till we all come in the unity of the faith,
and of the knowledge of the Son of God,
unto a perfect man, unto the measure of
the stature of the fulness of Christ:*

E very organization, corporate business, charity, school and even homes operate with rules. Most are written in policies, contracts and procedural documentations.   Depending   on   the

---

[6] E-Sword KJV

organisation and the regulations by which they must perform, there may be laws, acts and amendments.

Whatever the system, there are rules and there are bodies or groups to ensure that those rules, policies, procedures, regulations, acts, laws and amendments are adhered to.

The fact that these rules exist, they set a barrier or guide in place as to what should and what should not be done. The scripture tells us in Romans that if there were no law, then there would be no sin.

> **[7]Romans 7:7**   *What shall we say then? Is the law sin? God forbid. Nay, I had not known sin, but by the law: for I had not known lust, except the law had said, Thou shalt not covet.*

Ignorance we know is no excuse to the law, the fact that they are written rules and criteria by which to operate, going against them will find us in disobedience and out of alignment.

Going against workplace rules, could attract a caution or a disciplinary action in the workplace. If that is how man expects their rules, laws and amendments to

---

[7] E-Sword KJV

be adhered to, then how much more do we need to ensure that we always operate according to the laws of God.

God requires us to be obedient and in alignment with his will and word. We are his people and the sheep of his pasture, we are to move when he says move and stand still when he says stand still. We are expected to keep our lives and actions in accordance to the Word.

God has set out in his word the expectation and criteria by which we need to live. It is great to have expectations from God, the scripture tells us that the things we ask are supplied by him. Nevertheless, the things we desire from God must be aligned to his will and be in agreement with his word.

We cannot choose our own paths, start off in the wrong direction and then hope to arrive at the correct destination. We must ensure that we consult God all along the way and stay on the path ordered and directed by God.

The things we desire and expect to receive must be as God has pre-ordained, for only then will we be in alignment with his will. God's will for our lives have been detailed in his word. There are areas requiring more searching and seeking through prayer and fasting, devotion and dedication to God.

God has told us in his words that if we humble
ourselves, seek his face, and turn from our wicked ways
then and only then will he heal our land. We cannot go
through life from day to day behaving as though we are
the masters of our own destinies and we are
unaccountable. For we know that God will hold us
responsible for the things we fail to achieve, the souls we
fail to win and the action we fail to produce because we
have walked away from his will thereby rendering us out
of alignment.

Whatever it is then that we expect from God, it is
crucial that they are in his will.

The measuring plank for our alignment is Jesus
Christ. It is our aim to attain to his likeness, that of a
perfect man, unified in faith and the knowledge of Jesus
Christ.

[8]*Eph 4:13*   *Till we all come in the unity of the faith,
and of the knowledge of the Son of God,
unto a perfect man, unto the measure of
the stature of the fulness of Christ:*

---

[8] E-Sword KJV

Summary

Being aligned to God's will requires us to know what is his will for our lives. This will be discovered through spending time in his presence. We cannot simply rely on those who would tell us who we are in God, we must know for ourselves what it is that God has pre-ordained for us to be.

With full assurance, we can then live our lives knowing that we are in God's will, because he has provided us with inspiration, information, instruction and revelation.

CHAPTER 4

CHECK YOUR SUBSTANCE

What lies behind you and what lies in front of you are small comparisons to the greatness that lies within you

[9]Ephesians 1:17-19

Eph 1:17   *That the God of our Lord Jesus Christ, the Father of glory, may give unto you the spirit of wisdom and revelation in the knowledge of him:*

Eph 1:18   *The eyes of your understanding being enlightened; that ye may know what is the hope of his calling, and what the riches of the glory of his inheritance in the saints,*

---

[9] E-Sword KJV

Eph 1:19   *And what is the exceeding greatness of his power to us-ward who believe, according to the working of his mighty power*

O f course being aligned to God requires faith. For we are approaching a being that we cannot see with our natural eyes, nor hear with our natural ears. We won't be able to touch him with our hands, for God is Spirit (John 4:24) and he is not defined nor perceived through our sensory perceptions.

[10]Joh 4:24   *God is a Spirit: and they that worship him must worship him in spirit and in truth*

Faith then must become the overwhelming factor for anyone pursuing after God. What then is faith? Often when we are asked to define or describe what faith is. The overwhelming response is to quote [11]Hebrews 11:1, *"Now, faith is the substance of things hoped for the evidence of things not seen"* and we feel justified that we have set our Christian mentality at ease, because we have provided a biblical quotation as explanation to a question.

---

[10] E-Sword KJV

[11] E-Sword KJV

However, I have discovered that the knowledge and quoting ability of Hebrews 11:1, does not allow someone to truly grasp with full understanding, what faith really is.

Hebrews 11:1 states:

[12]**"Now faith is the <u>SUBSTANCE</u> of things hoped for..."**

The substance is the core element contained within, allowing it to operate. The matter within allows evidence of the thing to become visible. I like to think of faith as expectation, when I am expecting something, I get prepared for its arrival, I become positioned or postured to receive it.

According to Hebrews 11:1, faith is also described as "[13]...the <u>EVIDENCE</u> of things not seen"

A seed planted in the earth is covered by the soil. The unseen metamorphosis which takes place, after time; produces the evidence that something was happening in the ground, hidden away from view. The fact that it was not seen, does not hinder its mutation. The visible result

---

[12] E-Sword KJV

[13] E-Sword KJV

of a plant or tree stands as a testament or evidence that the invisible had taken place.

Another wonderful teaching of faith that will aid in understanding faith as a substance which produces evidence, is that of the mustard seed.

Matthew 17:20 and Luke 17:6 both provides a definition as given by Jesus about faith when he made the comparison of faith to that of a grain of mustard seed while teaching his disciples.

> [14]*Mat 17:20*   *And Jesus said unto them, Because of your unbelief: for verily I say unto you, If ye have faith as a grain of mustard seed, ye shall say unto this mountain, Remove hence to yonder place; and it shall remove; and nothing shall be impossible unto you.*

> [15]*Luk 17:6*   *And the Lord said, If ye had faith as a grain of mustard seed, ye might say unto this sycamine tree, Be thou plucked up by the root, and be thou planted in the sea; and it should obey you.*

---

[14] E-Sword KJV

[15] E-Sword KJV

Both these scriptures draw reference to the grain but it does not refer to the size of the mustard seed.

However, for decades I have heard this teaching, and often the speakers would allude to the *'size of the mustard seed'* as the key focus of the message Jesus was conveying. They encouraged the saints that no matter how 'small' the faith they possessed was, if they had faith any at all, though small, it should be able to move a mountain or command a tree to be plucked up and planted into the sea.

In some cases, the mustard seed has been called the smallest seed even though it is not the smallest seed, for there are indeed smaller seeds. Referring to these scriptures, the congregation is taught that no matter how *small* they perceive their faith to be, even if it is as small as a mustard seed, it will still work.

That teaching within itself is in some ways correct, howbeit, that is not what Jesus was teaching; and missing the information contained in his message, has caused the profoundness of the text to be lost.

Telling ourselves that our *little* or *small* faith should still work, our focus becomes the size of our faith, rather than the substance or core element necessary to manifest the evidence of our faith.

I do feel that I need to qualify the information provided regarding the smallest seed before I proceed. Found in tropical rain forests is the [16]Epiphytic orchid which produces the world's smallest seed. Compared to a mustard seed, it is noticeably smaller, in fact; it can barely be seen with the naked eye.

Summary

If we agree that the mustard seed is not the smallest seed, then Jesus could not have been referring to the size of the seed. For had his message been about the size of the seed, then he would have referred to the smallest seed that is in existence, and if anybody would know what was the smallest seed, Jesus would.

Since the focus of his message was nothing to do with the size of the mustard seed, it then stands to reason that we need to pay closer attention to the mustard seed itself.

I believe that should we take some time and investigate the mustard seed, its uses, its properties, how it grows, the tree it produces and such like, we would

---

[16] http://waynesword.palomar.edu/ww0601.htm#seed

realise that the text and indeed Jesus' message carries a much deeper and far greater meaning.

If we then take the information we have discovered about the mustard seed and apply that knowledge to faith, we will begin to grasp what faith really is with clearer understanding.

CHAPTER 5

THE MUSTARD SEED FAITH

What is in you will be evidenced by what comes out of you

[17]Mark 4:31-32

Mar 4:31   *It is like a grain of mustard seed, which, when it is sown in the earth, is less than all the seeds that be in the earth:*

Mar 4:32   *But when it is sown, it groweth up, and becometh greater than all herbs, and shooteth out great branches; so that the fowls of the air may lodge under the shadow of it.*

---

[17] E-Sword KJV

L et us now investigate 'a grain of mustard seed'. By so doing, it should paint a picture about the message Jesus hoped to convey to us when he taught his disciples, as recorded in the books of Matthew and Luke.

[18]Known as the *Cruciferae* or *Brassicaceae,* the Mustard family is from a large range of herbs. A plant with four petaled-flowers; it includes vegetables such as cabbage, cauliflower, broccoli, brussel sprouts, radishes, kale, watercress and turnips.
Mustard is known for its medicinal properties, it can be used for the relief of a sore throat and chest congestion, it is also used for its anti-inflammatory properties and in some cases has been known to relieve backache.

Mustard also has been used as a condiment, and as a spice to give flavor to foods and sauces. It has been used to make oil and there are some mustard trees which have leaves that are edible.

The mustard seed within itself has many uses and when paralleled with our faith, we will find that like the

---

[18] http://en.wikipedia.org/wiki/Cruciferous_vegetables
http://en.wikipedia.org/wiki/Brassicaceae

mustard seed, our faith should have healing and medicinal properties. The scripture tells us in James that if there are any sick among us, then let him call for the elders of the church who should pray over him, it encourages us to know that the prayer of faith shall save the sick and if he has committed any sin, it shall be forgiven.

[19]*Jas 5:14*   **Is any sick among you? let him call for the elders of the church; and let them pray over him, anointing him with oil in the name of the Lord:**

Jas 5:15   **And the prayer of faith shall save the sick, and the Lord shall raise him up; and if he have committed sins, they shall be forgiven him.**

Similarly, like the spice and condiment usage of the mustard, our faith is our flavour. Matthew 5:13 reminds us that we are the salt of the earth, the question posed is where would we be salted if we lose our savour? Our faith is our flavour and it gives the savour to our Christian lives. If we, as children of God lose our faith, then we are good for nothing.

[20]*Mat 5:13*   **Ye are the salt of the earth: but if the salt have lost his savour, wherewith shall it be salted? it is thenceforth good for nothing,**

---

[19] E-Sword KJV

[20] E-Sword KJV

but to be cast out, and to be trodden under foot of men.

One grain of mustard seed is enough to bring forth a great mustard tree. Unlike some trees which are indigenous to certain areas, the mustard tree is found practically everywhere in the world.

Our faith therefore, like the mustard tree should not be indigenous to any particular area, but instead be found no matter where we are in the world, no matter what situation we face and no matter what condition surrounds us. Our faith should be present.

I am not a gardener and I certainly do not have green fingers. Even if I receive a plant as a gift, I either water it too often, feed it too much or on the other extreme, I don't water it enough, so I am not knowledgeable about plants and seeds, without doing some research or speaking to a gardener. However, I found out that some plants and trees cannot be planted in close proximity to certain other plants or trees. Reason is, one may take on the attributes of the other. For example, I learned that tomatoes cannot be planted next to jalapenos, for the tomatoes will take on the characteristics of the jalapenos and you will reap "hot tomatoes".

However, because the mustard has a pungent characteristic, it can be planted anywhere, next to any plant or tree and still remain true to its nature. It is not affected by its surroundings and will not change to suit its environment.

This is how our faith should be. We should be able to apply our faith to any situation and our faith should bring transformation to the situation, instead of our faith be changed by the situation.

I attended a service in 2010 where a visiting speaker, Bishop C. A. Holdsworth from Jamaica was teaching on the mustard seed faith. [21]He taught that the mustard tree grows to a height of twenty-one feet in the air, however its roots grows three times as fast beneath the surface. Which means that a twenty-one feet high tree would have a root sixty-three feet deep.

Another thing to note is this; there is more of the tree in a place that cannot be seen, in the earth. Our faith then must be so deeply rooted in God, and being so deeply set, that we should be unmovable. Nothing should move our faith.

---

[21] http://markbeaird.org/steph/pdf/sermons/tim_dubberly/mustard_faith.pdf

Another alarming piece of information that Bishop Bosworth shared is this; he said that the mustard tree can grow to a width of seventy-two feet wide, when compared to our faith, our faith should be so wide in its impact that it reaches across every barrier, limitation and boundary and effect a positive response of faith in others.

One last thing I want to share about the mustard tree is from an article I read, written by [22]Tim Dubberly in 2004 which he extracted from a message by one brother Pylant.

It explained that the mustard tree is deciduous, it is not seasonal, it is evergreen. This means that it is not affected by the cyclical external conditions of the weather. It does not shed its leaves, it is consistent.

Even so should our faith be. Like the evergreen nature of the mustard tree, our faith should remain constant and flourish inspite of the conditions around us.

Summary

We can now agree that the message Jesus was trying to teach us through comparing faith to a grain of mustard

---

[22] http://markbeaird.org/steph/pdf/sermons/tim_dubberly/mustard_faith.pdf

seed, is much more profound in its meaning and holds a greater significance in its lesson.

It was never about the size of the mustard seed, but more so, the substance contained in the seed, which produces the resulting evidence of faith. The greatness of faith is not dependent on its size but the substance or the prepared expectation contained within the possessor of faith.

Faith, regardless of its size, must be identified, prepared and aligned. Faith then is the unwavering assurance that no matter what is going on around you, or what condition you have found yourself in; you wait expectantly, postured to receive what God has promised, regardless of how long it takes.

CHAPTER 6

THE EVIDENCE

Now hear the conclusion of the matter

[23]James 2:14, 17-18

Jas 2:14	*What doth it profit, my brethren, though a man say he hath faith, and have not works? can faith save him?*
Jas 2:17	*Even so faith, if it hath not works, is dead, being alone.*
Jas 2:18	*Yea, a man may say, Thou hast faith, and I have works: shew me thy faith without thy works, and I will shew thee my faith by my works.*

---

[23] E-Sword KJV

I have so many faith testimonies that I could share, with you, testimonies that stand as a demonstration of the substance which produces evidence. Following, I have shared one, this happened when my Vauxhall Vectra decided to pack up and I needed to get a new vehicle.

In March 2009, my family and I were at home and I was busy writing. I have the bad habit of staying up quite late, often alone in the still, quiet of the house, while everyone else is asleep. There, after resting and praying; I would normally embark on studying, researching or writing.

This particular night, I felt an urge for junk food and so I jumped in my car and proceeded to drive 2.75 miles from our home to a large supermarket.

After purchasing what I needed to keep me fuelled up for the break of dawn, I started to make my way back home. As I drove home, the car started to make noises that was a bit disconcerting and of course as I suspected, not long after there was a large bang as the fan belt gave out. Concerned I allowed it to roll as far as it would go and guided it out of oncoming traffic so that it would not be a hazard.

While this would have been an overwhelming experience, especially at 1:30am in the morning, the mercy of God allowed that the fan belt lasted until I was literally meters away from my house. Though a bit annoyed, I was grateful to God that he had allowed me to be walking distance from my home.

I simply called the recovery company, picked up my bags and walked safely home. I remember saying to God, well I know this is just the means by which you are going to bless me with a new car for you know Lord that my car is not a luxury but rather a necessity.

Needless to say, at that time we had not budgeted for another vehicle and this was not a discussion that my husband would have welcomed as we simply did not have the finance. However, I had the faith to know with assurance that due to the fact that my car was a necessity, God would not allow me to go for too long without a vehicle.

As a part of the coverage that I had taken with the recovery company was a free courtesy car for a number of days and without calling them, a wonderful car was delivered to my house for me to use, I was overjoyed. On sitting in the vehicle I was taken aback with its pilot like dash-board, the illusion that I was high off the road, though it is a hatchback and the many controls including music controls on the steering. Elated, I immediately said to God, God this is the car I need you to bless me with. I had identified my expectation.

Soon, without the finance to buy a car and without the credit to get a loan, I set off by faith to search for this particular vehicle. The amazing thing was, that model was a new make from the car company and with the MOT system (ensuring that cars are roadworthy), new cars are not due a MOT test until three years, therefore, I had a good two more years to wait before a second hand one would come onto the market.

Regardless of this, I continued my search, calling car companies, searching the web and a few would pop up as available but they were overseas. It seemed a long shot, and an impossible journey, but I had crazy faith and I knew that God would give me the desire of my heart.

Finally, there was a ray of light, one particular car company invited me to take a look at their car lot. On arriving he took my husband and I through the formalities and tried to get us to sign the paperwork to release the vehicle. While he spoke, turning up his charms and using his best sales man pitch, I kept looking through the glass doors to see my car, but it was not there. Frustrated I said to him, you do have the car I want don't you? To which he responded no, but I can take any car off their lot. He then proceeded in trying to sell me another type of vehicle, I heard myself saying to him, that's not God. Thanks but we will try somewhere else.

He looked at us as though we were crazy, for it was a long shot that another company would be willing to give us the loan. Nevertheless, we kept walking. On approaching the door, he began to tell us about another car supermarket that was much bigger and had a wider variety of cars on their lot or in their branches, located all over the country. We got the directions and off we went.

After taking many wrong turns we finally asked a pedestrian for direction and he pointed us in the right way. We arrived and just as the sales man had described, it was as though we had walked into a sea of cars. There were many cars, of all sizes, colours, shapes, makes and models, we knew we had arrived at the right place.

Confidently we walked in, and asked to speak to someone about buying a car. A stocky well-built man directed us to a seat and one of their sales representatives, a tall, well-dressed chap with hair slicked back in place came over to meet with us. He greeted us and asked what he could do for us. I began telling him that I was interested in only one car, the Toyota Auris and that he was to check his computer and see if there were any on site or at another location and then we could go from there.

He checked and lo and behold, there it was. On the computer screen in front of us, was a dark blue Auris, less than a year old that had just come on the market. It's owner had bought the car months previously and sadly passed away. I immediately said, that's my car.

He prepared the paperwork and God did the rest, a process which should have been impossible as we had no money or worthy credit, through faith became possible. Even with worthy credit, it would still be a seven day procedure, within three days I drove my new car off their premises and God has been faithful in keeping his word. It still runs like a dream.

I did not have the money, neither did my husband, but we had faith. Faith enough that what God promised he would provide and like Elijah who foretold of impending rain according to his word, and God backed him up; we walked in knowing that God would back us up and allow someone to agree our financing. Indeed I still give him praise for my car which I have affectionately named Favour.

Summary

Faith will produce evidence, faith will bring about results. The name it and claim it days are behind us, it is time to speak it and know that it is done, according to your word, because you have aligned your expectations with the Word of God, the result should be produced or manifested evidence.

Bibliography

E- Sword KJV

References

Information re the Mustard Seed

http://waynesword.palomar.edu/ww0601.htm#seed
http://en.wikipedia.org/wiki/Cruciferous_vegetables
http://en.wikipedia.org/wiki/Brassicaceae
http://markbeaird.org/steph/pdf/sermons/tim_dubberly/mustard_faith.pdf

ABOUT THE AUTHOR
More from **Dr Claudette King**

 Dr Claudette King is an author, bible teacher and seminar speaker. She along with her husband John, operate an online bible college which allow learners to gain insight into theological subjects from the convenience of their home; anywhere in the world.

With an internet connection, students can access the bible college and begin their theological journey.

Find out more about Dr King from her website, visit her today at www.drclaudetteking.com

A Wilderness Study
Doctoral: Christian Education in Administration & Organisation

Every athlete will testify that not finishing a race is one of the worst feelings they can have. For once started, the aim indeed is to finish, preferably in first place, but finish nonetheless. Like those running a race, when going through a wilderness experience, the determination to endure is what we need most.

This book will aid the reader to gain knowledge for those hard times. Providing detailed account of some such as Moses, the Children of Israel, David, Job, John the Baptist and Jesus, who have gone through wilderness experiences in their lives and have left us examples from which we can draw inspiration and learn. Take this journey and gather tools to aid you in enduring your wilderness.

Dr Claudette King

Gender*less* Anointing
There is neither male nor female

 This book takes the reader through the corridors of time introducing the societal and hierarchical status placed on women within the several social classes. An eye-opening investigation into the social customs, beliefs and practices encouraging Paul's writing. Spanning the bronze age and into the twenty-first century; its reader is provided with answers to age-old questions regarding the writings of Paul and the supposed silence of women.

Self-Publish
Without Breaking the Bank

This is a simple step by step comparison of what it could cost authors, musicians and film-makers to self-publish and what they could save should they follow the steps outlined in this very short book. Save money and galvanise your thoughts and ideas or music in print by becoming a published author, musician or film-maker today.

ORDER IN THE CHURCH SEMINAR
"Let all things be done decently and in order"
(1 Corinthians 14:40)

Whether you are a church leader, auxiliary head, minister, aspiring leader, church administrator, trustee or youth leader, this is for you.

'Order in the Church' is a thought-provoking seminar dealing with Administrative, Governmental, Ministerial and Spiritual Order.

Dr Claudette King is available to conduct this seminar at your assembly, do visit her website for more details.

ORDER IN THE CHURCH DVD & WORKBOOK

"Let all things be done decently and in order"
(1 Corinthians 14:40)

Want to hear the seminar but not able to have Dr King come to you, then why not purchase the DVD and workbook today? The DVD is of an actual session taught with the accompanying workbook, you will feel you are in the session. Complete your workbook, pause and rewind and repeat as many times as you desire to grasp clearer understanding on any of the areas taught.

Not sure what to expect, you can view a video clip of what people thought of the seminar. To view the video and find out more about the seminar, visit her website www.drclaudettking.com. All products are available from her website.

18988599R10033

Made in the USA
Charleston, SC
01 May 2013